JV PUBLICATIONS

MARKETING BLUEPRINT

WHY VIRAL ARTICLE MARKETING GENERATES LIST BUILDING SUCCESS – EVERY TIME

Jan Verhoeff

ABSTRACT

List driven marketing to your key niche buyers in a direct list connection always trumps splatter or mass marketing options, regardless of the intensity of the marketing strategy. How you build your list matters, because it designates the power you have to attract their attention and compel them to take action, based on means and method. In this document, you'll find not only mass appeal and comprehension of the process, but grasp a firm understanding of the power that comes from list development.

Legal Disclaimers

The ideas and suggestions in this book are all tried and true, used frequently and often by people mentioned in these pages, who may or may not be familiar with this Publication. If they're in this book, I've visited their sites, marketed their work, appreciated their talents, or helped them create their online brand in one way or other. That does not mean I know the amount or quality of their success, their business, or their online money making values, but simply that they are using one of the many ways I would use to make money online – and I do recommend others use these methods as well.

I make no assumptions or promises of the impact or success you will have as a business owner if you do any of these items. Your success is up to you and none is implied or guaranteed in this document.

Please do not presume this to be tax, legal, or any other professional recommendation or service and hire such professionals as you need in your business. This document provides only ideas and what you do with those ideas is up to you.

As of this publication – all websites are visible and active, businesses are currently viable and all details are as close to factual and specific as we can make them, for more information about any one business or to hire my services as a business consultant – please contact me using contact information near the back of the book.

ISBN-13: 978-1508440338
ISBN-10: 1508440336

(this page intentionally left blank)

MARKETING BLUEPRINT – THE SECRET OF VIRAL ARTICLE MARKETING AND LIST BUILDING SUCCESS

Advertize your Business with Viral Article Marketing strategies keep your readers coming back time after time to your recognized brand. Brand effective marketing drives traffic and your readers begin to recognize your writing style when they see it. Give them prime examples, every time you write.

1 - GENERATE A STELLAR TRAFFIC-DRIVING TITLE

No matter what else your title does for your article, it must drive traffic. If you can't figure out if it drives traffic or not, look at how many hits you get from the article. You want a title that if they don't do anything besides click the title, they still find the link.

2 - AUDIENCE CAPTURING SUB-HEADERS

Keep the sub-headers simple, but specific enough to tell the reader what they need to do. Give yourself some leeway here, and use audience grabbing words. Action words speak louder than passive phrases. Get specific with your sub-headers and tell the reader what they'll learn.

Write as if you're speaking directly to a person. Grab their attention with tonal changes, verbs that speak out loud, and directives that are understood to be meant for them. Don't hesitate to get personal. If you know your reader isn't listening to you, TELL THEM.

Make your articles flow from part one (title) to the ending (click through link). You want your reader to see the last step just as certainly as they saw the title. Make your resource box a part of your article and keep them reading through the last line.

5 - GENERATE SHOW STOPPING HOOKS

The advantage of catching your reader off guard with a pertinent choice is that they make the easy choice first. If you allow your reader to opt out - they will. Don't give them that option until AFTER they opt in. Tell them what to do in clear language that grabs their click.

6 - USE KEYWORD ADVANTAGE

By using your recognized branding phrases in your articles, your readers become familiarized with them and begin to search those phrases on the Internet Search Engines. Create keyword phrases that brand your website and products to your own advantage in the articles you write.

Give your readers a reason to click the links provided in the resource box. Tell them what they'll get and ensure they'll click by making it easy for them to understand the process. Use the whole value marketing technique of systemic advertizing with relevant content.

BONUS: CALL TO ACTION

How do you maximize your online income? These three high-impact marketing strategies will power up your income and generate highly targeted traffic to your website.

When you started building your business, you had a great idea, it fell into place rather rapidly and now you're waiting for something great to happen. The winds might change and blow a few ship loads of traffic your way, or you could actively entice relevant targeted traffic your way using these three high-powered marketing strategies.

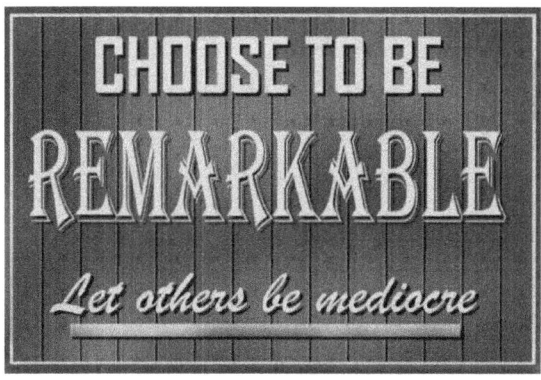

Capture their attention with headlines that draw them to read what you write.

IF your headline lacks power and substance they won't take the time to see if your copy has anything to offer. They'll hit that x in the corner and delete it. Powerful, emotion grabbing words in your headlines will capture their attention and focus their interest on your articles.

RELEVANT CONTENT WITH INTERESTING FACTS WILL KEEP THEM READING AND PERSUADE THEM TO READ MORE OF YOUR ARTICLES.

When you write with action terms that convince your reader that you do know what you're talking about, they want to read more. Passive words bring passive readers. Action oriented terminology increases the temperature in your copy, compels the reader to continue reading through your words, and keeps their attention riveted on your content.

Always include a call to action at the end of your article.

Invite them to keep reading with a question that says there's more to come, offer them something more at your website and tell them to go there. A call to action is the most necessary part of your article.

Do you have the Secret Solution to Online Marketing Strategies?

Claim your FREE Subscription to Secrets to Prosperity Solutions at http://secret2prosperity.com

DOS & DON'TS OF ARTICLE MARKETING

Audience grabbing articles drive profit and revenue. Topic is insignificant in today's marketing world, and yet, your topic will make or break your Internet Business.

CONSIDER FOR A MOMENT, YOUR TOPIC IS GLAMOUR TIPS FOR HOME BASED BUSINESS MAVENS...

If your article marketing centers on just dress code, you'll lose the war on marketing in the infrastructure of high fashion. However, if you concentrate on marketing your style-conscious efforts on work at home moms with a flair for simplicity, your article marketing efforts may be highly rewarded with high ranking pages and article titles. Do you recognize the difference?

Do - write creative articles within your topic with high-interest titles that focus on keyword phrases your readers will search frequently.

Don't - write predictable articles that reiterate last week's press releases from some other business.

Do - provide quality content, marketable information, and necessary information for the market.

Don't - lose focus and ramble your way through the article with no apparent direction or motive for writing.

Do - generate innovative NEW information broadcasts that elevate your topic to PRESS RELEASE status and capture the audience.

Don't - regurgitate insignificant mutterings your readers won't listen to and don't want to hear.

Do - focus on positive influential reviews, studies and how-to information that grabs attention and reveals potential opportunity.

Don't - attempt to suck your reader into the article with a great title that leaves them wondering what you had in mind as you ramble through nana land in your article.

Do - write enticing, power-charged titles that magnetically attract readers.

Don't - reject reader interest with a boring, do-nothing title that falls flat on the paper.

Do - promote product, services and information.

Don't - make the mistake of self-promotion in your articles. This deadly error will lead your readers to the EXIT.

Do - market your article efforts on social networks and spread the wisdom through quick message alerts.

Don't - limit your articles to back street magazines and Ezine hideaways with no visibility.

Creating a marketable approach to article marketing strategies is an effective way of presenting your business to a broader audience. If you have not attempted to persuade your market successfully through article marketing, the suggestions you'll find below are valuable.

Visit http://advertizeyourbusiness.com to learn efficient clarification of article marketing opportunities and how you can apply these to your business. You'll have opportunity to claim two FREE article marketing templates and a FREE Subscription to ADvertiZe eZine an important part of any Internet Business Marketing Effort.

ABOUT THE AUTHOR

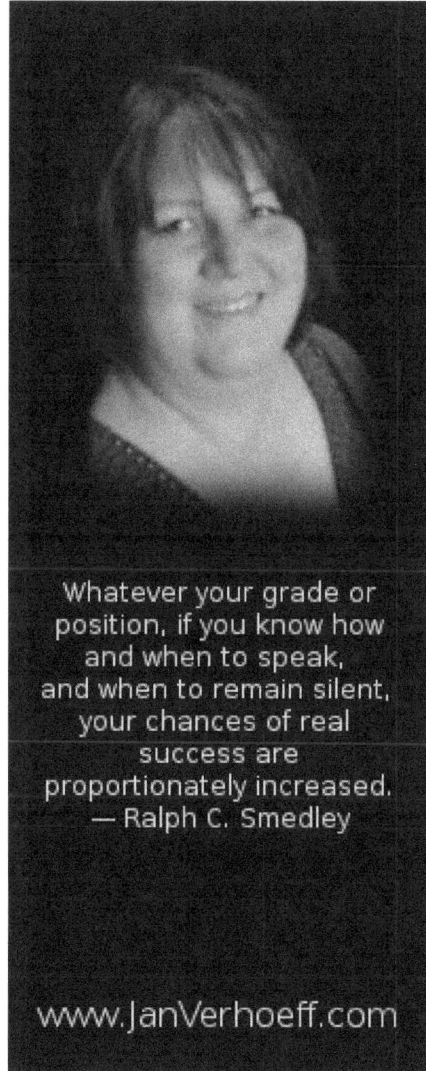

Whatever your grade or position, if you know how and when to speak, and when to remain silent, your chances of real success are proportionately increased.
— Ralph C. Smedley

www.JanVerhoeff.com

Jan Verhoeff offers expertise in online marketing, writing, copywriting and brand recognition. She presents logical, sound marketing knowledge that will drive your business profits from an online presence. Her motto for success is, "Generating profit and global recognition for local businesses."

What you get when you work with Jan Verhoeff:

<u>Brand Recognition for your business online.</u> Jan goes beyond teaching to help you achieve recognition for your brand online, attracting business and a global market to your web site, your product and your services.

<u>Expert Marketing knowledge to lead your business to profits.</u> Jan takes the initiative to drive your market niche to profits using more than three decades of experience in marketing.

Copywriting experience to build your presence online. Jan understands how the search engines work to drive traffic to small business sites, creating a funnel of profits into your business on the web.

Keynote speakers for your events. Jan knows the importance of creating and hosting powerful marketing events for small businesses. She has developed a list of connections with recognized keynote speakers who specialize in business development, internet commerce and global economics.

❖ Whether your event is in a local coffee shop or college lecture hall, or a massive conference center, Jan has the perfect keynote speaker in mind.
Contact jan@janverhoeff.com for details.

Inter-office training for social marketing development of your business is available at selected points around the nation. Jan Verhoeff creates events, sets up speakers and organizes marketing for group training events, specializing in Social Marketing Management for small business owners. Your social marketing budget does not have to eat up your profits.

Learn how you can increase new business development, e-commerce training and marketing, as well as increase social media impact for your business online. Strategic marketing methods taught by Jan Verhoeff will impact your profit margin and increase brand recognition for your business online.

❖ For an effective business evaluation and strategy session – contact Jan@JanVerhoeff.com

RESOURCES

http://inetmoneymachine.com

http://janverhoeff.com

Jan does quality work. She's always accessible and easy to reach. She makes time in her busy schedule for time sensitive matters. Jan has great integrity and does beautiful work, I highly recommend her as webmaster for your website.

Janice Deardorff

* * *

Jan is a talented and skillful marketing coach. Her clients realize significant gains in their businesses and their incomes. I highly recommend Jan and her services!

Hugh Liddle, CEO

Red Cap Sales Coaching

* * *

Jan is one terrific website designer and an extremely creative and gifted writer. I am getting great responses to my newly launched website that she designed, and I am beyond proud of it, and finding working with her immensely rewarding. How could I know that my REAL life's work would begin at age 74??

Bob Troy